Cheep!

...se is ... ior you. It is full of good

This ...okes to tell your dad, your mum, your baby brother, your teacher and anybody else you can think of.

Actually, you don't *have* to have a sense of humour to buy this book. The main thing is the money. If you are short of money, you could buy the book with a friend and have a half each; or 96 friends and have a page each; or 15,682 friends and have a word each.

On the other hand, if you have plenty of money, you could buy two copies and laugh twice as much. If you are a millionaire, you could buy them all and make the publisher laugh.

This seems like a good book!

Look over

Come on up

What goes
Ha Ha Bonk?

I feel funny

Any pear
jokes in this
book?

I feel bunny

A man laughing his head off

THE
HA HA BONK
BOOK

Janet and Allan Ahlberg

PUFFIN BOOKS

Come on everybody!

Let's read the rest of it

I'm stopping here

PUFFIN BOOKS

Published by the Penguin Group
Penguin Books Ltd, 80 Strand, London WC2R 0RL, England
Penguin Putnam Inc., 375 Hudson Street, New York, New York 10014, USA
Penguin Books Australia Ltd, 250 Camberwell Road, Camberwell, Victoria 3124, Australia
Penguin Books Canada Ltd, 10 Alcorn Avenue, Toronto, Ontario, Canada M4V 3B2
Penguin Books India (P) Ltd, 11 Community Centre, Panchsheel Park, New Delhi – 110 017, India
Penguin Books (NZ) Ltd, Cnr Rosedale and Airborne Roads, Albany, Auckland, New Zealand
Penguin Books (South Africa) (Pty) Ltd, 24 Sturdee Avenue, Rosebank 2196, South Africa

Penguin Books Ltd, Registered Offices: 80 Strand, London WC2R 0RL, England

www.penguin.com

First published 1982
Published simultaneously by Viking
059

This collection copyright © Allan Ahlberg, 1982
Illustrations copyright © Janet Ahlberg, 1982
All rights reserved

Printed in Great Britain by Clays Ltd, St Ives plc

ISBN-13: 978–0–140–31412–0

www.greenpenguin.co.uk

MIX
Paper from
responsible sources
FSC
www.fsc.org   FSC™ C018179

Penguin Books is committed to a sustainable
future for our business, our readers and our planet.
This book is made from Forest Stewardship
Council™ certified paper.

Is this a long book?

Contents

I'm tired already

Tell me a joke!

I'll race you

Wait for me!

Morning!

Jokes to tell your Dad

Dads are busy men. If you want to tell your dad a joke, choose a good time. For instance, catch him early in the morning while he is still in bed. Don't be put off if he pulls the blankets over his head.

If you miss him in bed, get him in the bathroom. Try shouting jokes to him through the keyhole or under the door.

Dads like jokes about football, elephants, wooden legs and Englishmen, Irishmen and Scotsmen. Here are some you can try.

Give me a piggy back

Who's the boss of the hankies?
The hankie chief.

How do you know when there's
an elephant under your bed?
Your nose touches the ceiling.

Knock, knock!
Who's there?
Cook.
Cook who?
That's the first one
I've heard this year.

Doctor, doctor, my wooden leg
is giving me a lot of pain.
Why's that?
My wife keeps hitting me over
the head with it.

Why is getting up at three o'clock
in the morning like a pig's tail?
It's twirly.

HERE IS A TRAIN ANNOUNCEMENT
The train now arriving on platforms
5, 6, and 7 is coming in sideways.

Did you hear about the well-
behaved little boy?
Whenever he was good, his dad
gave him 10p and a pat on the
head. By the time he was sixteen,
he had £786 and a flat head.

What was the tortoise doing
on the motorway?
About ten yards an hour.

But his teeth stayed in

What happened to the man who couldn't tell toothpaste from putty?
All his windows fell out.

How can you keep cool at a football match?
Stand next to a fan.

BARBER: How would you like it, sir?
MAN: Could you cut it very short on one side and not at all on the other, with a sort of crooked fringe at the front and big tufts pulled out at the back?
BARBER: Oh dear, I don't think I can manage that, sir.
MAN: Why not? You did last time.

What's wrong with a man with jelly in one ear and sponge cake and custard in the other?
He's a trifle deaf.

I'm a piggy for trifle

10

What's green, lives in a field
and has 4,000 legs?
Grass – it was a mistake about
the legs.

Did you hear about the two flies
playing football in a saucer?
They were practising for the cup.

BOY: My dad plays the piano by ear.
GIRL: So what? My dad fiddles with
his whiskers.

Who was the father
of the Black Prince?
Old King Cole.

How can you tell which end
of a worm is his head?
Tickle him in the middle and
watch where he smiles.

Excuse me

What do you give a sick bird?
Tweetment.

What do you give a sick pig?
Oinkment.

What do you give a sick lemon?
Lemonade.

Where would you weigh a whale?
At a whale-weigh station.

How did the sailor know
there was a Man in the Moon?
He went to sea.

Why did the girl keep a loaf
of bread in her comic?
She liked crummy jokes.

12

Two biscuits were walking down
the road. One got run over.
What did the other one say?
'Crumbs!'

One day in the jungle there was a
football match between the elephants
and the insects. By half-time the
elephants were winning 39-0. Then
in the second half a centipede came
on to play for the insects. He was
a brilliant player. The elephants
could find no way to stop him, and
by the end of the match the score was
46-39 to the insects.

As they were leaving the field,
the captain of the elephants said,
'What puzzles me is, why didn't you
play that centipede in the first half?'

'We would have,' said the captain
of the insects. 'The only trouble
is, it takes him an hour to get his
boots on!'

I know
the problem

How can you stop an elephant
from smelling?
Tie a knot in his trunk.

How do you know when there's an
elephant in your bed?
You can see the 'E' on his pyjamas.

Why couldn't the two elephants
go swimming?
They only had one pair of trunks.

Why is an elephant big, grey
and wrinkly?
Because if he was small, white
and round he'd be an aspirin.

Doctor, doctor, my hair's coming
out. Can you give me something
to keep it in?
Certainly – how about a paper bag?

Sorry—full up

DOCTOR: Have you had this before?
MAN: Yes.
DOCTOR: Well, I'm sorry to say
you've got it again.

What's grey, has four legs
and a trunk?
A mouse going on holiday.

What's brown, has four legs
and a trunk?
A mouse coming back from holiday.

Did you hear about the boy
who was christened $6\frac{7}{8}$?
His dad picked the name out
of a hat.

15

What did Tarzan say when he saw
the elephants come over the hill?
'Here come the elephants!'

What did Jane say when she saw
the elephants come over the hill?
'Here come the grapes!' She was
colour-blind.

zzub zzub

You're going
the wrong
way

I want
my mummy

Jokes to tell your Mum

Mums are busy women. For instance, if your mum is the Prime Minister, she has to run the country. If she is the Queen, she has to run the country as well, *and* make Prince Philip's sandwiches. The Queen, by the way, likes jokes about horses, wooden legs and Englishwomen, Irishwomen and Scotswomen.

One more thing: mums are supposed to be the experts on children; but this is not always so. After all, who else do you know who gets you up in the morning when you're sleepy, and sends you to bed at night when you're wide awake?

What happens when the Queen burps?
She issues a royal pardon.

BOY: Do you notice any change in me?
MUM: No. Why?
BOY: I just swallowed 5p.

Knock, knock!
Who's there?
Orson.
Orson who?
'orse and cart.

If two's company and three's
a crowd, what's four and five?
Nine.

What's grey, has four legs
and weighs one and a half tons?
A fat mouse.

I'm getting off
this page!

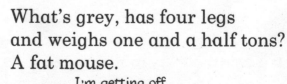

A lady went into a pet shop.
'I want a parrot for my little
girl,' she said.

'Sorry, madam,' said the shop-
keeper. 'We don't do swops.'

Pretty Polly

What did the first mind-reader
say to the second mind-reader?
You're all right, how am I?

Why do golfers take an extra pair
of trousers with them?
In case they get a hole in one.

Did you hear about the boy
who had Egyptian flu?
He caught it from his mummy.

Atishoo!

WOMAN: Did you just save my
little boy from drowning?
MAN: Yes, madam, I did.
WOMAN: Well, where's his cap?

Knock, knock!
Who's there?
Amos.
Amos who?
A mosquito just bit me.

Knock, knock!
Who's there?
Andy.
Andy who?
And he bit me again.

What did the judge say
to the dentist?
Do you swear to pull the tooth,
the whole tooth and nothing
but the tooth?

Left, right,
left, right!

One day a little boy was playing in
the garden when he tore his trousers.
His mum told him to take them off
and she would mend them.

'But stay in your room till I've
finished,' she said.

Some time later she heard a noise
in the garden. Thinking the little
boy had left his room, she called out,
'You bad boy – are you running around
out there without any trousers on?'

At that moment the gas man appeared.
'No, madam,' he said. 'I've just come
to read the meter.'

How do you make an apple puff?
Chase it round the garden.

Doctor, doctor, people
keep ignoring me.
Next, please!

BOY: Where are you going, Mum?
MUM: To the doctor's. I don't
like the look of your sister.
BOY: I'll come with you. I don't
like the look of her either.

Me neither

Who's that at the door?
The Invisible Man.
Tell him I can't see him.

Who's that at the door?
A man with a drum.
Tell him to beat it.

Who's that at the door?
A man with a wooden leg.
Tell him to hop it.

Who's that at the door?
A woman with a pram.
Tell her to push off.

How rude!

How do you hire a horse?
Put four bricks under him.

MUM: Why are you crying?
BOY: Dad hit his thumb with a hammer.
MUM: Knowing you, I'm surprised
you didn't laugh.
BOY: That's the trouble – I did!

A wonderful bird
Is the pelican.
His beak holds more
Than his belly can!

Why should you never tell
secrets in a greengrocer's?
Because potatoes have eyes
and beanstalk.

... so I says
to her......

What's yellow and stupid?
Thick custard.

Where does a sick ship go?
To the dock.

Jokes to tell your Baby Brother

Baby brothers like jokes about English babies, Irish babies and Scots babies. So do baby sisters. Babies, in fact, like jokes about anything. This is because they cannot tell one joke from another.

If you want to practise your jokes, try telling them to a baby. Babies are good listeners. They do not tell you to go away and read a book. They are never too busy, or on the phone, or just going out.

So, if you have a baby in the house, tell him a joke. If you run out of jokes, make rude noises. He will like that even more.

What should you do if a child
falls down a well?
Get a book about bringing up
children.

Well
well
well

There was once a baby who was very
quiet. He never said 'Mama' or
'Dada'. He never said anything.
When he was three he still hadn't
said anything, and his mum and
dad were worried. When he was five
he *still* hadn't said anything and
they were more worried than ever.

Then, one day when he was having
his dinner, he said, 'Not enough
salt!'

'Goodness me,' said his mum.
'You can talk! Why is it all these
years you've never said anything?'

'Well,' said the boy, 'you see,
up till now everything's been all
right.'

26

What did the big chimney
say to the little chimney?
You're too young to smoke.

What did the big telephone
say to the little telephone?
You're too young to be engaged.

What did the big candle
say to the little candle?
I'm going out tonight.

What did the traffic light
say to the car?
Don't look now, I'm changing.

What should you do if a baby
swallows your biro?
Use a pencil.

HERE IS A NEWS-FLASH
A lorry-load of wigs has been
stolen on the M1. The police
are combing the area.

Why is an old car like a baby?
It never goes anywhere without
a rattle.

Shall I tell you the joke
about the high wall?
I'd better not. You'll never
get over it.

Where did Humpty Dumpty put his hat?
Humpty dumped 'is 'at on the wall.

Ooo-err!

THIS
IS
A
NOTICE

Humpty Dumpty sat on the wall.
Humpty Dumpty had a great fall.
All the King's horses
And all the King's men
Said, 'Scrambled eggs for dinner again!'

HERE IS ANOTHER NEWS-FLASH
A 4-foot man and a 9-foot man
have just escaped from jail.
The police are looking high
and low for them.

Hello
hello
hello

Where does the baby monkey sleep?
In the apricot.

What did the earwig say
as he fell off the wall?
Earwig go again!

THIS
IS
NOT
A
NOTICE

Why can't a man's head
be twelve inches wide?
Because if it was,
it would be a foot.

Are you a bat
or an umbrella?

Yes

Is it
safe?

30

Jokes to tell
your Best Friend
and your Worst Enemy

If your best friend is a boy, he will like jokes about ghosts, vampires and monsters. If your best friend is a girl, she will like jokes about vampires, monsters and ghosts. If your best friend is a vampire, he won't have much time for jokes.

Your worst enemy will also like jokes about ghosts, vampires and monsters; but the joke is, you don't tell him any. If your *worst enemy* is a vampire, watch out!

Help!

How does a witch tell the time?
With a witch watch.

'Just think,' said the boy,
'a big strawberry ice-cream,
two bags of crisps and a front seat
at the pictures – all for 10p!'
   'Wow!' said his friend.
'Did you get all that for 10p?'
   'No,' said the boy. 'But just
think!'

Knock, knock!
Who's there?
Isabel.
Isabel who?
Is a bell necessary
on a bicycle?

Who did Dracula marry?
The girl necks door.

I can make you talk
like a Red Indian.
How?
See, I told you!

BOY: What's the difference between
a rhinoceros, a lemon and a tube
of glue?
GIRL: I don't know.
BOY: Well, you can squeeze a lemon
but you can't squeeze a rhinoceros.
GIRL: What about the tube of glue?
BOY: I thought that's where you'd
get stuck.

Doctor, doctor, I feel like
a pair of curtains.
Pull yourself together, man!

What animal do you look like
when you have a bath?
A little bear.

Oh –
what's this?

Shall I tell you the joke
about the body-snatchers?
No. You might get carried away.

Shall I tell you the joke
about the empty house?
There's nothing in it.

Shall I tell you the joke
about the butter?
I'd better not. You'll only
spread it.

Daddy, daddy, there's a spider
in the bath!
Don't worry, you've seen spiders
before.
Yes, but this one's four feet wide
and it's using all the hot water!

I thought
this was
a funny
book

I'm scared

What did the father ghost say
to his son?
Spook when you're spooken to.

DRACULA'S SCHOOL REPORT
Reading: good
Writing: untidy
Cricket: shows
promise as a bat.

Where was grandma when
the lights went out?
In the dark.

Why couldn't the skeleton
go to the dance?
He had no body to go with.

Doctor, doctor, I feel like a bridge.
What's come over you, man?
Well, so far two cars, three lorries
and a bus!

GIRL: Last night I had to get up
and open the door in my nightie.
BOY: That's a funny place to have
a door.

How do you start a teddy bear race?
Ready, Teddy, go!

How do you start a flea race?
One, two, flea!

How do you start a jelly race?
Get set.

How do you start a pudding race?
Sago!

That's
a fairy
tale

What happened to the girl who slept
with her head under the pillow?
The fairies took all her teeth away.

Knock, knock!
Who's there?
Felix.
Felix who?
Felix my ice-cream,
I'll lick his.

The sausage is a cunning bird
  With feathers long and wavy,
It swims about the frying pan
  And makes its nest in gravy.

What lives at the bottom
of the sea with a shotgun?
Billy the Squid.

A friend
of mine

37

Knock, knock!
Who's there?
Banana.
Banana who?
Knock, knock!
Who's there?

Banana.
Banana who?
Knock, knock!
Who's there?
Banana.
Banana who?
Knock, knock!
Who's there?
Orange.
Orange who?
Orange you glad I didn't
say 'banana'?

Why did the tap dancer have
to retire?
He kept falling in the sink.

What happens when pigs fly?
The price of bacon goes up.

What's frozen water?
Ice.
What's frozen cream?
Ice-cream.
What's frozen tea?
Iced tea.
What's frozen ink?
Iced ink.
Well, have a bath then!

If a red house is made of red bricks,
and a blue house is made of blue
bricks, what's a green house made of?
Glass.

Why is it cheap to feed
a giraffe?
A little goes a long way.

There were two Bishops in a bed.
Which one wore the nightie?
Mrs Bishop.

What is the best thing
to put into a pie?
Your teeth.

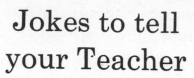

Careful

Jokes to tell your Teacher

Teachers like jokes about reading, writing and arithmetic. They also like jokes about happy, carefree teachers having cups of tea in the staffroom – and school holidays.

If your teacher asks you a question and you do not know the answer, tell her a joke instead. It will cheer her up. Your teacher needs cheering up. After all, she is stuck in a classroom with *you* five days a week. Also, you only have to go to school till you're sixteen; teachers have to go till they're sixty!

I like cups of tea too

My dad can fight your dad

SCHOOL→

A teacher was talking to a new boy
in her class.

TEACHER: What's your name?

BOY: Let's see...Happy birthday
to you, happy birthday to you,
happy birthday dear Brian...it's
Brian, miss!

TEACHER: If you add 387 and 769,
then double it and divide by 5,
what do you get?

BOY: The wrong answer, miss.

Where did Napoleon keep
his armies?
Up his sleevies.

How do you spell 'hungry
horse' in four letters?
M T G G.

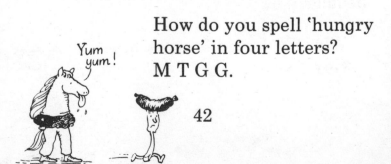

Yum
yum!

What do misers do in cold weather?
Sit round a candle.
What do misers do in very cold
weather?
Light it!

Brrr—
it's me
again

Why couldn't the sailors play cards?
The captain was standing on the deck.

MUM: Come on, John, eat your breakfast;
you'll be late for school.
JOHN: I don't want to go to school.
The teachers don't like me, the children
don't like me – even the caretaker
doesn't like me!
MUM: All the same, you must go.
JOHN: Why should I?
MUM: Well, for one thing you're forty-five
years old, and for another you're the
headmaster!

What exams do farmers take?
Hay levels.

My feet
hurt

Why can't you starve at the seaside?
Because of the sand which is there.

TEACHER: If you had 10p, and you
asked your dad for another 10p,
how much would you have?
BOY: Er, ... 10p, sir.
TEACHER: You don't know your
arithmetic, boy!
BOY: You don't know my dad, sir.

What should you know if you
want to be a lion tamer?
A bit more than the lion.

Why do bees hum?
Because they don't know the words.

What do you get if you cross
an elephant with a kangaroo?
Big holes all over Australia.

What do you get if you cross
a sheep with a kangaroo?
A woolly jumper.

What do you get if you cross
a cow with a duck?
Cream quackers.

What do you get if you cross
a cockerel with a poodle?
A cockerpoodledo!

mmm mmm poo mmm

What do you get if you cross
an owl with a skunk?
A bird that smells but doesn't
give a hoot.

BOY: I think my teacher loves me.
GIRL: How can you tell?
BOY: She keeps putting kisses by
my sums.

I eat my peas with honey;
　　I've done it all my life.
It makes the peas taste funny,
　　But it keeps them on the knife.

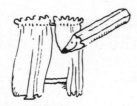

Why did the girl take
a pencil to bed?
To draw the curtains.

TEACHER: Tell me an animal
that lives in Lapland.
BOY: A reindeer, sir.
TEACHER: Good! Now tell me
one more.
BOY: Er..., another reindeer!

Whosoever
this shoe fi
shall be m
bride

What did the one ear say
to the other ear?
Between you and me, we need
a haircut.

*Two lips —
get it?*

What flowers grow under your nose?
Tulips.

TEACHER: If I had ten oranges in
one hand, and seven in the other,
what would I have?
GIRL: Big hands, miss!

What can you do if a herd of
elephants comes racing towards
you?
Make a trunk call and reverse
the charge.

A teacher was taking her class
for a walk in the woods.

'Now, Mary,' she said. 'What do
we call the outside of a tree?'

'I don't know, miss,' said Mary.

'Bark, you silly girl,' said
the teacher. 'Bark!'

'Oh, all right then,' said Mary.
'Woof-woof!'

Marry me

48

I've lost
my shoe

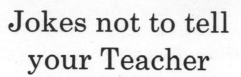

Jokes not to tell your Teacher

Most teachers enjoy a good joke, otherwise they wouldn't be teachers. All the same, don't tell your teacher jokes about naughty children getting caned by *their* teacher; it might give her ideas.

One more thing: never tell your teacher a joke when she is eating her dinner. She might start coughing and hit you in the eye with a bit of boiled potato, or – worse still – spray you with a mouthful of semolina. And that's *no* joke!

That's nothing—
I've lost my
leg

That's
nothing—
I've lost
my
head

GIRL: Please, sir, I wish we
lived in the olden days.
TEACHER: Why?
GIRL: Then there wouldn't be
so much history to learn.

There once was a schoolboy called Kidd,
Who ate twenty pies for a quid.
When they asked, 'Are you faint?'
He replied, 'No, I ain't,
But I don't feel as well as I did!'

What's the difference between
a nail and a bad boxer?
One's knocked in and the other's
knocked out.

Did you know Davy Crockett
had three ears?
A right ear, a left ear
and a wild frontier.

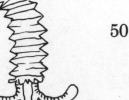

50

TEACHER: What came after the
Stone Age and the Bronze Age?
GIRL: Please, sir – the sausage!

Once upon a time there was a donkey.
This donkey lived in a field by the
side of a river. On the other side
of the river there was another field
full of delicious carrots. The donkey
wanted the carrots but the
river was too deep for him to wade,
too wide for him to swim, and there
was no bridge. The donkey didn't have
a boat and he couldn't fly. So how
did he get across?
    Do you give up?
    That's all right – so did the donkey.

TEACHER: If you had 40p in
one pocket and 55p in the other,
what would you have?
BOY: Somebody else's trousers, sir.

I've got
somebody else's
trousers on

What goes chuff-chuff
at a wedding?
The bride's train.

TEACHER: How do you spell 'wrong'?
BOY: r, o, n, g, miss.
TEACHER: That's wrong!
BOY: Good, I got it right, then.

 What's the difference between
a bottle of medicine and a doormat?
One's shaken up and taken;
the other's taken up and shaken.

Knock, knock!
Who's there?
Boo.
Boo who?
There's no need to cry,
it's only a joke.

I hate these
knock knock
jokes

Why did the fly fly?
Because the spider spied 'er.

Why did the owl 'owl?
Because the woodpecker
would peck 'er.

Why didn't the viper
vipe 'er nose?
Because the adder 'ad
'er 'andkerchief.

TEACHER: You're late! You should
have been here at nine o'clock.
BOY: Why, miss – what happened?

What's the difference between
a church bell and a robber?
One peals from the steeple;
the other steals from the people.

I steal from
the steeple

I peel from
the peel

TEACHER: Your hands are very dirty, girls. What would you say if I came to school with hands like that?
GIRLS: We'd be too polite to mention it, miss!

54

Hello hello hello

Jokes to tell
your Milkman,
Dustman, Postman,
Policeman

Policemen like jokes about handcuffs, truncheons and panda cars.

Milkmen like jokes about milk, cream, cheese, butter, yoghurt, eggs, orange squash and Christmas hampers.

Postmen like all jokes, except the ones about big dogs chasing postmen.

Dustmen don't like any jokes. They think they're just a load of rubbish.

I think I'm being watched

What's wrong with rubbish?

Pooh.

Where do policemen live?
Letsby Avenue.

A man rushed into a bank and
pointed his finger at the cashier.
'This is a muck-up!'
    'Don't you mean "stick-up"?'
said the cashier.
    'No,' said the man, 'muck-up
– I forgot my gun.'

Who gets the sack as soon
as he starts work?
A postman.

What happened to the robber
who pinched a bar of soap?
He made a clean getaway.

Wheeee

What goes 99 bonk?
A centipede with a wooden leg.

Why did the orange stop
at the top of the hill?
It ran out of juice.

Forth from his den to steal he stole.
His bags of chink he chunk.
And many a wicked smile he smole,
And many a wink he wunk.

What did the policeman say
to his tummy?
You're under a vest.

What's short, green and goes
camping?
A boy sprout.

Doctor, doctor, I keep thinking
I'm a spoon.
Well, sit there and don't stir.

Doctor, doctor, I keep thinking
I'm a billiard ball.
Well, get back in the queue.

Doctor, doctor, I keep thinking
I'm a pack of cards.
Sit down. I'll deal with you later.

What does the ocean say when
it sees the shore?
Nothing, it just waves.

A postman limped into a hospital.
'A dog's bitten my leg!' he said.
   'Oh dear,' said the nurse. 'Did
you put anything on it?'
   'No,' said the postman. 'He
liked it just as it was.'

58

Why did the burglar cut the legs
off his bed?
He wanted to lie low for a while.

What's bread?
Raw toast.

Knock, knock!
Who's there?
Cows go.
Cows go who?
No – cows go moo!

Got any spare milk?

FIRST MAN: Have you seen a
policeman round here?
SECOND MAN: No.
FIRST MAN: Do you know where
the nearest police-station is?
SECOND MAN: No.
FIRST MAN: Right, then –
stick 'em up!

Looks
eggsciting over
here

How do hens and roosters dance?
Chick to chick.

Cheep
to cheep

Did you hear the joke
about the three eggs?
No?
Two bad.

Why are cooks bullies?
They whip the cream
and beat the eggs.

They batter
the fish
too!

What goes over the water,
under the water,
on the water
and yet never touches the water?
An egg in a duck's tummy.

What's yellow and white
and gets eaten at 100 m.p.h.?
A train driver's egg sandwich.

The Eggs-press

What did the egg say
in the monastery?
Oh well, out of the frying-pan
into the friar.

Knock, knock!
Who's there?
Egburt.
Egburt who?
Egg but no bacon.

Hello! Hello!

There were two eggs in a pan of
boiling water.
  'Wow,' said the first egg, 'it's
getting hot in here!'
  'That's nothing,' said the second.
'Wait till they get you outside;
they'll bash your head in with a spoon!'

What does the Spanish farmer
say to his chickens?
Olé!

Eggs-periment

What do policemen like best
in their sandwiches?
Truncheon meat.

What do you get if you cross
a snowball with a shark?
Frostbite.

Who was the fastest runner?
Adam. He was first in the
human race.

What's green, hairy and
goes up and down?
A gooseberry in a lift.

What's yellow and dangerous?
Shark-infested custard.

You should
be on the other
page

No-we're the
eggs-tras!

Knock, knock!
Who's there?
Irish stew.
Irish stew who?
I arrest you in the name
of the law.

Double Ducks

Doctor, doctor, I keep thinking
there's two of me.
One at a time, please.

Copy Cats

What do you call a sleeping bull?
A bull-dozer.

What's purple and hums?
An electric plum.

Why did the boy throw the clock
out of the window?
To see time fly.

What did the ear 'ear?
Only the nose knows.

Is this
a short cut?

Rrrrringgg!

Jokes to tell
your Mother-in-Law

If you are a girl, your mother-in-law is your husband's mother. If you are a boy, your mother-in-law is your wife's mother. Of course, if you are a boy or a girl, you probably haven't got a mother-in-law. In which case, you may have to save these jokes for a while.

Or...you could tell them to your *mother's* mother-in-law. Your mother's mother-in-law is your grandma. Your father's mother-in-law is your other grandma. Your auntie's sister's uncle's cousin by her second marriage twice removed, has got nothing to do with it.

Stop pushing!

Mother-in-Law —
I thought this
was a kid's book!

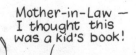

Who's Santa Claus's wife?
Mary Christmas.

A tramp went to a lady's house
for something to eat.
   'Would you mind eating yesterday's
soup?' said the lady.
   'No,' said the tramp.
'Good!' said the lady. 'In that
case, come back tomorrow.'

A man having dinner at Crewe
Found a small hairy mouse in his stew.
Said the waiter, 'Don't shout
And wave it about,
Or the others'll want one too.'

Why don't elephants like penguins?
They can't get the paper off with
their trunks.

Mary had a little lamb,
   Who had a sooty foot.
And into Mary's bread and jam,
   His sooty foot he put.

What's bad-tempered
and goes with custard?
Apple grumble.

What's big, red and eats rocks?
A big red rock-eater.

Why can't you play cards
in the jungle?
Too many cheetahs.

DOCTOR: You should live to be eighty.
MAN: I am eighty!
DOCTOR: What did I tell you?

What cake gives you
an electric shock?
A currant bun.

What lies at the bottom
of the sea and shivers?
A nervous wreck.

One day a big tortoise, a middle-
sized tortoise and a little tortoise
went into a café. They ordered
three banana splits. While they were
waiting, they noticed it had begun
to rain.

'Look at that,' said the big
tortoise. 'We should have brought
our umbrella.'

Borrow my
umbrella

68

'You're right,' said the middle
tortoise. 'Let's send the little one
back to get it.'

'I'll go,' said the little tortoise.
'Only you must promise not to eat
my banana split while I'm away.'

Well, the big tortoise and the
middle-sized tortoise did promise,
and so the little tortoise set off.

A few days later the big tortoise
said to the middle tortoise, 'Come on,
let's eat his banana split anyway.'

'All right then,' said the middle
tortoise.

At that moment the little tortoise
shouted back from the end of the
café, 'You do that, and I won't
fetch the umbrella!'

What flies and wobbles?
A jellycopter.

I'm lost

What goes up the drainpipe down,
but won't go down the drainpipe up?
An umbrella.

Why did the girl take
a hammer to school?
It was breaking-up day.

What's white on the outside,
green on the inside and hops?
A frog sandwich.

wheeeeeee

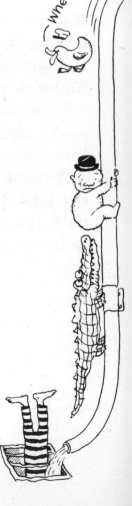

70

Jokes to tell
your Dog

If you want to tell your dog a joke, choose a hot day. This way the dog will look as though he's laughing, whether he finds it funny or not.

Dogs like jokes about cats and lamp-posts; also bones; also other dogs who go into public houses and order pints of beer.

If the dog growls while you are telling the joke, it means he's heard it before. If he bites your leg, he probably has no sense of humour.

Excuse us
please

Two cats were looking at a bird in a cage.
  'That's not a canary,'
said the first cat. 'It's green.'
  'You never know,' said the second.
'Maybe it's not ripe yet.'

Why did the dog wear black boots?
His brown ones were at the menders.

What does the hedgehog
have for his lunch?
Prickled onions.

Why does the ocean roar?
Well, wouldn't you if you
had crabs on your bottom?

Did you hear about the sheep
dog trials?
Three of the dogs were guilty.

What bet can never be won?
The alphabet.

DOCTOR: You need glasses.
MAN: But I'm already wearing
glasses.
DOCTOR: In that case, *I* need glasses.

What do you call a gorilla
with a machine-gun?
Sir!

What happened to the man
who stole a calendar?
He got twelve months.

What stands still and goes?
A clock.

How can you stop your dog from
barking in the back garden?
Put him in the front garden.

Let the dog......

What's green and goes
boing-boing-boing?
Spring cabbage.

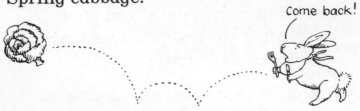

Come back!

Why does the rabbit have
a shiny nose?
Because her powder puff
is on the wrong end.

What's the difference between
a crazy rabbit and a forged
pound note?
One's a mad bunny; the other's
bad money.

..... see the
rabbit

wheeeeeeee!

Wheeee!

Wheeeee!

Wheeeee!

Wheeeee!

What do you get if you pour
boiling water down a rabbit hole?
Hot cross bunnies.

Knock, knock!
Who's there?
Lettuce.
Lettuce who?
Let us in and you'll find out.

Yum yum!

Did someone
mention
lettuce?

TEACHER: If I gave you three rabbits,
then the next day I gave you five
rabbits, how many would you have?
GIRL: Nine, miss.
TEACHER: Nine?
GIRL: Yes, miss. I've got one already.

If a cat dressed up as a cowboy
went into a saloon with his arm
in a sling, what would he say?
'I'm looking for the man who shot
my paw!'

What four letters frighten robbers?
O I C U.

What's worse than finding
a maggot in an apple?
Finding half a maggot.

When are sheep like ink?
When they're put in a pen.

Why did the farmer drive the
steam-roller over his field?
He wanted to grow mashed potatoes.

Sausage and
mash!

Did you hear about the man
who bought a paper-shop?
It blew away.

It's dog's delight
    To bark and bite,
And little birds to sing
    And if you sit
    On a red-hot brick,
It's the sign of an early spring.

A man went into a pet shop.
'Do you have any dogs going cheap?'
'No, sir,' said the shop-keeper.
'All ours go "bow-wow".'

What should you do if you find
a gorilla in your bed?
Sleep somewhere else.

What lies down a hundred
feet in the air?
A centipede.

Waiter, waiter, what do you
call this?
It's bean soup, sir.
I don't care what it's been –
what is it now?

Home
Sweet
Home

Jokes to tell
somebody else's Dog

If the dog you tell your joke to is an English dog, an Irish dog or a Scottish dog, you will probably get a laugh. If it's a French or German dog, you could have trouble being understood.

By the way, never pull faces at strange dogs. The dog won't mind, but the owner might think you're pulling them at him.

Another thing: if you visit a zoo, always remember this: a hyena is not a dog, though it will laugh at anything. Wolves are not dogs either, though they will sometimes pretend to be just to gain your confidence. But watch out! They will eat you up – *and* your grandma!

Let's have a rest

Good idea

What is the difference between
a dog and a flea?
A dog can have fleas;
a flea can't have dogs.

What's the difference
between a duck?
One of his legs is both the same.

What's the difference between a
well-dressed man and a tired dog?
The man wears a suit; the dog
just pants.

What's the difference between
a drink of tea and a magician?
One's a cuppa; the other's a sorcerer.

Why couldn't the butterfly
go to the dance?
It was a moth ball.

Doctor, doctor, I keep thinking
I'm a dog.
Lie down on this couch and I'll
examine you.
I can't. I'm not allowed on the
furniture.

I keep
thinking I'm
a dog

How did Little Bo-Peep
lose her sheep?
She had a crook with her.

Where do you find
the youngest soldiers?
In the infantry.

What did the baby sardine say
when he saw a submarine?
Look, mum – a tin of people!

One day a postman came to a house.
He found a big, barking dog on
the doorstep.

'Don't worry,' said the lady.
'You know the old saying: "A
barking dog never bites".'

'Yes,' said the postman. 'I know
the old saying. You know the old
saying. What bothers me is – does
the dog know the old saying!'

TEACHER: Name four animals
of the cat family.
BOY: Father cat, mother cat,
...and two kittens!

What happens if you put a cat
in a washing-machine?
You get a sock in the puss.

WAITER: What will you have, sir?
MAN: Steak and kiddly pie, please.
WAITER: You mean steak and kidney pie, sir.
MAN: I said kiddly, diddle I?

Ahhhh!

What happened to the cat
who swallowed a ball of wool?
She had mittens.

What's purple and burns cakes?
Alfred the Grape.

What's black and white and black
and white and black and white?
A penguin rolling down a hill.

What's black and white
and red all over?
A shy zebra.

Waiter, waiter, there's a fly
in my soup!
Don't worry, sir, that spider
on your bread will get him.

Waiter, waiter, do you call
this a three-course meal?
Yes, sir: two chips and a pea.

Waiter, waiter, you've got
your thumb in my soup.
That's all right, sir. It's
not hot.

Are we
nearly there
now?

Jokes to tell Yourself

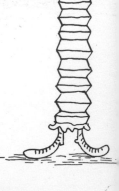

I'm very tall

The jokes you tell yourself will depend on the kind of person you are.

For instance, if you are a busy person, you may have to come back later or phone yourself up. If you are very tall, you may have to stand on a chair. If you haven't got a sense of humour, you won't laugh anyway. On the other hand, if you've heard the joke before, you'll probably have to hear it again.

Have you heard this one?

Pardon?

How did the monkey make toast?
He put it under the gorilla.

Knock, knock!
Who's there?
Little old lady.
Little old lady who?
I didn't know you could yodel.

There was an Englishman, an Irishman
and a Scotsman. One day they were out
walking and came to a cave. Inside
the cave there was a table, and on
the table there was a pound note.
The trouble was, the cave was haunted.

Well, first the Englishman crept
in and tried to get the pound note.
But just as his hand reached out a
spooky voice said:

'I'm the ghost of Auntie Mabel.
That pound note stays on the table!'

So then the Englishman screamed with
fright and ran off.

I like this
joke

Next the Irishman crept in and tried
to get the pound note. But again,
just as *his* hand reached out, the
spooky voice said:

'I'm the ghost of Auntie Mabel.
That pound note stays on the table!'

So then the Irishman screamed with
fright and ran off.

Last of all, the Scotsman crept in.
But once more, just as *his* hand
reached out, the spooky voice said:

'I'm the ghost of Auntie Mabel.
That pound note stays on the table!'

But then – instead of screaming
with fright – the Scotsman said:

'I'm the ghost of Davy Crockett.
That pound note goes in my pocket!'

And he ran off with it.

If there were two elephants
in a Mini, what game would
they be playing?
Squash.

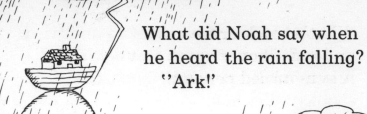

What did Noah say when
he heard the rain falling?
"Ark!"

What's the difference between a wet
day and a lion with tooth-ache?
One's pouring with rain; the other's
roaring with pain.

What do jelly babies wear
in the rain?
Gumboots.

Quack — march!

Why do birds fly south
in the winter?
It's too far to walk.

Can I come
under your
bucket?

I'll go
rusty

What's black and white
and red all over?
A sun-burned penguin.

How do you get rid of
water on the knee?
Wear drain-pipe trousers.

It's dry up here

What goes up when the rain
comes down?
An umbrella.

What do you call an Eskimo's cow?
An Eskimoo.

Where do snowmen dance?
At the snowball.

Yippee!

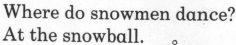

What goes dot-dot-dot-croak?
A morse toad.

What goes putt, putt, putt,
putt, putt, putt, putt, putt?
A bad golfer.

What goes, 'Quick-quick!'?
A duck with the hiccups.

Doctor, doctor, I've lost
my memory.
When did it happen?
When did what happen?

Why did the boy swallow 25p?
It was his dinner money.

What did the spaceman see
in his frying pan?
An unidentified frying object.

What's mad and goes to the moon?
A loony module.

Knock, knock!
Who's there?
Cornflakes.
Cornflakes who?
I'll tell you next week;
it's a cereal.

I wish I was a little grub
    With whiskers round my tummy.
I'd climb into a honey pot
    and make my tummy gummy.

Doctor, doctor, my little boy's
swallowed a bullet. What shall I do?
Well, for a start, don't point
him at me.

How far can a pirate ship go?
15 miles to the galleon.

What do you call a camel
with three humps?
Humphrey.

THE END

Is that
it then?

I still want
my mummy

Where do
we go
now?

SOLD

I'm worn out

Have a
cup of tea

Hey—there's
more books
over here!

I'm going to read Miss Brick

Hay the Horse sounds good

Some more books written by
Allan Ahlberg

HAPPY FAMILIES

Mr Biff the Boxer
Mr Cosmo the Conjuror
Mrs Plug the Plumber
Mrs Wobble the Waitress
Master Salt the Sailor's Son
Miss Jump the Jockey
Mr Buzz the Beeman
Mr Tick the Teacher
Mr and Mrs Hay the Horse
Mrs Lather's Laundry
Master Money the Millionaire
Miss Brick the Builder's Baby
Mr Creep the Crook
Miss Dose the Doctor's Daughter
Mrs Jolly's Joke Shop
Master Bun the Baker's Boy

Each Peach
PEAR Plum

TO
THE TRAIN

The winner!

Knock knock!

Who's there?

Toodle

Toodle who?

Bye!

Wait for us!

Oh!